THE NEED TO KNOW LIBRARY™

EVERYTHING YOU NEED TO KNOW ABOUT

CONFRONTING RACIST BEHAVIOR

LISA A. CRAYTON

Rosen
YA
New York

Published in 2019 by The Rosen Publishing Group, Inc.
29 East 21st Street, New York, NY 10010

First Edition

Library of Congress Cataloging-in-Publication Data

Names: Crayton, Lisa A., author.
Title: Everything you need to know about confronting racist behavior / Lisa A. Crayton.
Description: New York : Rosen Publishing, 2019 | Series: The need to know library | Includes bibliographical references and index. | Audience: Grades 7–12.
Identifiers: LCCN 2017045728| ISBN 9781508179153 (library bound) | ISBN 9781508179245 (pbk.)
Subjects: LCSH: Racism—United States—Juvenile literature. | United States—Race relations—Juvenile literature.
Classification: LCC E184.A1 C698 2019 | DDC 305.800973—dc23
LC record available at https://lccn.loc.gov/2017045728

Manufactured in the United States of America

On the cover: Racism is a problem around the world. This anti-racism protest took place in Melbourne, Australia.

CONTENTS

INTRODUCTION

Kayla (not her real name) dreamed of becoming a writer. She wanted to be a journalist who wrote for newspapers, but she also liked the idea of exploring new media. Inspired by her dream, Kayla attended an all girls' public high school located more than two hours away from home. She felt the long commute by bus and train was well worth the hands-on education she'd receive.

Nestled in a middle class, predominately white part of town, the school boasted a mostly minority student body. Many of the residents welcomed the students. Others did not. As an African American teen who had grown up in a racially diverse neighborhood, Kayla was not especially concerned. That all changed during her freshman year.

On Halloween, as Kayla and other students left school a group of masked Caucasian boys threw eggs at them. The boys yelled racist words at them. Dodging the eggs was not an option. With egg yolk clinging to their clothing, Kayla and the other girls raced back inside. They reported the incident to administrators. They stayed on the premises until the boys left and the police arrived. The scary ordeal was Kayla's first encounter with racist behavior. It would not be her last.

In an ideal world, race relations would always be peaceful. People would live in harmony. They would respect, perhaps even appreciate, the differences of other races. Schools, workplaces, and other local, national, and international venues would be safe for all and free from racial tension. People everywhere know the world is not ideal—and race relations are far from peaceful or harmonious!

Rather, racism is an age-old issue that continues to plague the United States and other nations. Racism thrives because there are people who believe that one race is superior to other races. That is the basic meaning of racism. This simplistic definition, however, does not capture the magnitude of the problem.

Racism is wrong. It causes unequal treatment. It affects housing, education, employment, health care, and other areas. Racist behavior comes in many forms. Ridicule and other verbal attacks demean those who are forced to hear them. Violence is used to scare and hurt activists. Other victims of racism are killed simply because they belong to the supposed "wrong" race.

None of these facts likely surprise you. Racism remains a hot topic in the news. Even those who do not routinely tune into such reports have seen racist behavior or have been the victims of racist behavior. Others, sadly, carry out such cruel acts.

Will racism ever end? The answer varies depending on who is asked. Many pessimists believe the issue is likely to exist forever. Optimists argue that there is hope for an end of racism. Some people just wish it to disappear. Wishing racism away has not ended it. However, confronting it results in positive change. More can be done. You can help.

Participating in peaceful protests with other teens and adults is an effective way to confront racist behavior in one's community.

Love is stronger than

While many concerned teens want to be involved, some mistakenly believe they have nothing to offer. One reason: the super-hero myth. Some teens look at their abilities, measure them against fictional characters, and feel inadequate. Why? In make-believe worlds, superheroes always save the day. Good beats evil. Peace reigns. Always.

The real world does not operate like that. Rather, conflict is con-stant. Peace and harmony are often short-lived. What a frustrating reality! At the same time, there are many opportunities for teens to get involved. They can join the fight against racism by con-fronting racist behavior. Conviction, commitment, and action are needed.

CHAPTER ONE

THE RACE CARD

Today's teens are among the most diverse in the history of our nation. The US government tracks race by several key categories. Those racial categories are white, Hispanic, black, Asian, American Indian/Alaska Native, Hawaiian or other Pacific Islander, and multiracial. According to the US Department of Health and Human Services (HHS) in 2014, the racial breakdown of American youth ages ten to nineteen, was as follows:

- White: 54.1%
- Hispanic: 22.8%
- Black: 14.0%
- Asian: 4.7%
- American Indian or Alaska Native: 0.9%
- Hawaiian or Other Pacific Islander: 0.2%
- Multiracial: 3.4%

By 2050, HHS projects the number of white youth will drop to 40.3 percent. The numbers of Black and American Indian/Alaska Native adolescents will also

The increasing diversity of the population makes it essential that people learn how to accept others' differences.

drop. However, the numbers of Hispanic, Asian, and multiracial young people will rise. Meanwhile, the number of Hawaiian or other Pacific Islander youth should remain the same.

JUDGE NOT!

As the racial makeup of the nation changes, it will be increasingly important to accept others' differences. "Don't judge a book by its cover" is an adage that encourages people to not make snap judgments. Most people have heard it numerous times growing up. It is good advice to follow in a lot of situations, including race relations.

Racism is the belief that one race is better, superior, and preferred over another. It is rooted in snap judgments. People treat others unfairly because of what they see—another person's race as reflected in their skin tone, hair texture, facial features, and other race-based characteristics.

Racism is evil. It has reared its ugly head for centuries and continues today. Time and history have proven that racism will not simply disappear. While there has been great progress, more is needed to improve current race relations.

BEYOND BLACK AND WHITE

Racism impacts people who have been born in a country and those who move there and later become citizens. Refugees also experience racism. Refugees are people who migrate to a country for various reasons. Religious persecution, war, and other factors force people to flee their homelands. Undocumented immigrants are others who suffer from racism. In America, these individuals often immigrate for many of the same reasons that refugees do.

Visitors also face racism while traveling to other states for business or pleasure. This is one reason the National Association for the Advancement of Colored

The United States and Canada have been a safe harbor for people fleeing from Syria and other countries where religious persecution, war, famine, or other harsh conditions are commonplace.

People (NAACP) issued a warning for blacks traveling to Missouri throughout the month of August 2017. It was the first time ever that the well-known civil rights organization issued an advisory for a whole state. Americans also face racism abroad, as do citizens of other countries who visit the United States.

When you consider the many groups that racism affects, it is clear that the problem is widespread. Victims in each category include people of all ages. It's also worth remembering that even people who have experienced racist behavior directed at them or at groups they are a member of can be guilty of racist behavior toward others. Why would anyone act this way? Because in their hearts and minds, people often believe they are better than their peers. Clearly, racism makes no sense. That is a fact teens need to understand while confronting racist behavior.

TYPES OF RACIST BEHAVIOR

Racist behavior can be subtle or overt. Such actions fall into four groups: unintentional, intentional, institutional, and internal.

Unintentional actions are not deliberate. People may not even know they are reacting in a certain way. A familiar example is when whites speed up when they see a group of minority teens. They are not trying to hurt the teens' feelings and may not even be think about why they have suddenly become nervous.

Intentional racism is obvious. Racist words or actions demean people of other races. Calling a person a racial slur is an example of this type of behavior. Placing racist symbols, like a noose or swastika, is another.

Institutional racism dictates what is acceptable in society. One example would be saying classical music is an authentic genre of music, but rap is not.

Meanwhile, internal racism happens when oppressed people hate their own race. Self-hate causes many people to make racist comments against other people of their race.

SOCIALLY ACCEPTABLE?

Social media is filled with words and pictures that bring people together—and tear them apart. Many people think their words, memes, and photographs are harmless. Other people disagree when those things show other races in a negative light. Just because a person says something is "only a joke" does not make a racist message OK.

If your social media is filled with friends' views and images that are racist, people will assume you are, too! Don't be labeled something you are not. Rather, help confront racism. There are four useful ways to do so.

First, share positive words and images that spark unity. Second, talk with friends about their tasteless messages. Third, remove people who repeatedly promote racism from your social media. And, fourth, report other people's racist social media messages.

UNDERSTANDING MICROAGGRESSIONS

Microagressions are a form of subtle racist behavior. They can be difficult to pinpoint. Sometimes microaggressions leave people scratching their head saying, "Did that really happen?," "What did that guy really mean by that?," or "Was that racist, or am I just easily offended?"

Microagressions include asking to touch another person's hair or making other inappropriate comments about its length or texture—don't do it!

Because of their subtleness, people of color may experience microagressions without realizing it. For example:

- White people marvel at your hair length, texture, or style.
- Strangers ask to touch your hair.
- People make comments like "You speak so well."
- People assume you like activities, food, movies, or other items simply because you are a member of a certain race or culture.

- Others repeatedly question your race because of your name, facial features, or other characteristics.
- Peers say you do not act like other people of your race.
- Without your permission, classmates give you nicknames because "your name is too hard to pronounce."

WHAT'S IN A NAME?

Names are Important. They are based on many factors. Some reflect a person's racial, cultural, or ethnic background. Others are based on a family's religion. Some are passed down from generation to generation. For these reasons and more, every person deserves for his her name to be treated with respect and dignity.

While some names may be hard to pronounce, teens show respect and foster acceptance when they use people's names correctly. More so, teens confront racism when they step in and tell others not to engage in racially charged name-calling. What can you do? Ask people how to pronounce their names and practice saying them properly. Refuse to call other teens by racially charged nicknames that make fun of them or their race. Don't laugh when other teens mock a teacher's name, in or out of the classroom. Help other teens understand that racist name-calling is never OK.

IMPROVING A NATION

Bullying and hate crimes are intentional racism. Because they are so harmful, it is important to identify and confront them. Racially charged bullying happens when someone makes threats, ridicules, or physically attacks another person because they are of a different race. It could also include making fun of a person's inability to speak English well.

Hate crimes can be verbal, written, or physical. These are some of the scariest forms of racist behavior. Hate crimes are serious crimes that carry greater

Tell a trusted adult if you experience racist behavior at school, even if the perpetrator is an educator. Holly Frye got involved after her son D. J.'s teacher used a racially charged term in class.

penalties than other crimes. They are sometimes committed by members of hate groups, such as the Ku Klux Klan (KKK).

The Southern Poverty Law Center (SPLC) tracks the number of hate groups operating in the United States. These groups target people for a variety of reasons, including race. In September 2017, the SPLC reported an astonishing 917 active hate groups! Does that shock you? It should.

It should also make it clear that confronting hate is vital. When it comes to racism, identifying all types of behavior enables teens to confront it at school, at home, and in other places in the community. Also, identification provides a path to self-reflection so that teens who are perpetuating such crimes can stop.

No one is born a racist, and racist behavior is learned. People who openly confront racism may experience pushback from family and friends. Nonetheless, their efforts are needed. They help spark improvements in cities, states, and nations.

CHAPTER TWO

HERE, THERE, EVERYWHERE!

Middle school students in Michigan taunted their classmates with the racist words "Build the wall! Build the wall!" while in the cafeteria. They referred to President Donald Trump's controversial proposal to build a wall along the border between the United States and Mexico.

White hate groups assembled in Virginia to protest the planned removal of a monument to a Confederate general. A racist rammed his car into the crowd. He killed a white female activist there to protest the hate groups' gathering.

In North Carolina, someone painted "Black lives don't matter and neither does your vote" on a wall. The words slammed the value of black votes, saying that blacks are unequal to whites. Not so! They also referred to the Black Lives Matter Movement, which is dedicated to fighting racial profiling and other behavior.

To many Americans, these incidents represent examples of heightened racial tension in the nation. It may seem as if the United States is going backward in race relations. While that is an arguable point, it is certain that some people believe they can conduct racist behavior without any consequences. That is not true. Equally, it is not true that America is alone fighting a war on racism. Rather, across the globe, countries are battling racist behavior by individuals and groups who want to perpetuate fear and intimidation.

WHERE IT HAPPENS

Indeed, a sad fact about racism is that it occurs everywhere people meet. No place is exempt. People encounter racism everywhere in the community. In the workplace, employees face racism in hiring and promotion. At school, teens encounter racism from other teens who call them names, ridicule their hair, skin color, or

Racism is a global issue. Activists attended this rally in Melbourne, Australia, to counterprotest an event supporting racism and fascism (government by dictatorship).

language. At home, family members can hear racist jokes and doctrine that spew hate. Some parents even forbid their children to marry people of other races!

WHY IT HAPPENS

It is difficult to imagine why people would ever engage in racist behavior. There is no single answer. Rather, multiple factors contribute to a global problem. These include feelings of superiority, ignorance, tradition, world affairs, and hatred.

There is no such thing as a superior race. Every person of every race, therefore, deserves the right to live and thrive without being subject to racist behavior. Civil rights and human rights supporters have long believed

Young people involved in an interracial relationship may encounter resistance from their parents who do not want them to date a person of a different race.

this and confronted racism in the hopes of making this an everyday reality in the United States and abroad.

Racists believe differently. White supremacy groups like the KKK, for example, contend that whites are superior to all other racial groups. Thus, they use fear, intimidation, and violence to suppress nonwhites.

In the past, they have especially targeted blacks. But they believe all minorities are inferior to whites, and therefore do not deserve respect. Many racists actually believe the world would be better if only one race—theirs—inhabited it. Of course, that is not true. No race has the right to be in charge of the entire world, dictating limitations on other people or killing them.

Ignorance also fuels racism. Ignorance may include wrong ideas held about a particular group or lack of knowledge about people of other backgrounds. It is easy to correct ignorance, but some people who commit racist acts have no interest in acquiring information about another race. They'd rather base their attitudes and actions on assumptions. This is how prejudice starts and why it is so damaging.

THE IMPACT OF TRADITIONS

Many families have traditions that they keep to celebrate their family, culture, or country of origin. These are special times designed to be happy meetings. In this respect, tradition is a good thing.

Conversely, traditions based on racism are not good. Unfortunately, there are families who pass down to new

ON THE CALENDAR

Throughout the year, there are holidays that honor different races and cultures. Some of these are celebrated in the United States. Others are observed around the world. Celebrating these unique holidays helps teens confront racism by developing an understanding and appreciation of a different race and its contributions to society.

Parades, arts performances, school assemblies, religious programs, museum exhibits, and many other activities mark these holidays. Some families also have special meals and invite family and friends to observe these special days on the calendar.

Some of these holidays are as follows. For specific dates, check a current calendar. Also do an online search for other countries' holidays. You may find some you'd like to know more about and/or celebrate.

- Black History Month (February)
- Chinese New Year (January or February)
- St. Patrick's Day (March 17)
- Asian Pacific American Heritage Month (May)
- Cinco de Mayo (May 5)
- Philippine-American Friendship Day (July)
- National Hispanic Heritage Month (September 15–October 15)
- National Native American Indian Heritage Month (November)

generations a legacy of racism and hatred. For example, one photo from a 2017 rally hosted by a white supremacist group went viral. It showed a little white girl dressed in a hooded garment similar to those worn by the KKK. From her attire, it was obvious, the girl was being reared in a tradition of racism. Teens who are members of such families often face stiff opposition when attempting to confront racist behavior.

World affairs including war also spark racism or are tied to racism. Fear is another root cause. Contributing factors of fear include ignorance, tradition, or hatred of a certain race. Indeed, hatred is a key factor shaping much racist behavior.

Stephanie Sinnot (*center*) faced pressure at home because of her work with best friend Mareshia Rucker (*right*) to integrate their school's prom.

One thing is clear: many of the causes of racism are interconnected. Sometimes they cannot be separated from each other. This is why racism can be difficult to end.

It is possible that you can think of other reasons that you have been a victim of racist behavior or someone you know has been. You do not have to suffer such behavior. And you can be an agent for change!

MYTHS AND FACTS

MYTH: To really address racism, a teen must be color-blind.

FACT: Trying to ignore or be blind to another person's race actually is not beneficial, or needed. Rather, truly accepting people of different races helps you see, acknowledge, and celebrate their race.

MYTH: If my family members are involved in racist behavior, I can never confront it.

FACT: You can choose to be different from your family members. Make up your own mind how you want to treat people of other races. If family members make racist jokes or comments, call them out on it and let them know that you don't agree with or approve of that kind of talk.

MYTH: Special holidays for certain races are not needed.

FACT: Black History Month and other special holidays are needed. They help reduce ignorance, a key factor causing racism. They also help promote acceptance, tolerance, and inclusion.

CHAPTER THREE

ROOTS OF CONFLICT

The roots of our nation's racial conflict date back to the early days when Europeans arrived on this side of the Atlantic Ocean. English settlers arrived in what is now Jamestown, Virginia, in 1607. As expected, the newcomers found native people there.

In 1492, more than a hundred years before the first European settlers arrived at Jamestown, Christopher Columbus first stepped ashore in the Americas. He and his crew traveled from Spain and were surprised to find a New World and its inhabitants. The natives were likewise surprised by the unexpected arrival of the Spaniards.

The challenges were many. But the primary one was that they did not speak each other's languages. Language became the first barrier to communication. Nonetheless, it was clear that the natives enjoyed a rich culture, healthy lives, an established religion, and flourishing land. Those were signs of a fully developed culture. Yet in those early encounters, something strange happened. Columbus and the crew felt superior. They

A protest occurs in front of a statue of Christopher Columbus. In recent years, activists have argued the Columbus Day holiday ignores how his actions led to the mistreatment of Native Americans.

considered the natives savages. By what measure did the Spaniards base their opinion? Language, cultural, and racial differences.

Those differences were used as a foundation for widespread racism. Millions of native people were killed during European "conquests." Others died due to new diseases introduced into the population by Europeans. Native people did not have immunity to those illnesses, which did not exist in their lands before. The native population dramatically shrunk.

RACISM AGAINST BLACKS

Fast forward to 1607. When the English settlers arrived, they, too, adopted an attitude of superiority that fueled racism. They grew tobacco and other crops. Initially, indentured servants provided labor. But more workers were needed. In 1619, twenty Africans arrived by ship in Jamestown. They had been kidnapped from their homeland. They were forced to come to Virginia and work as slaves under cruel conditions. Millions of Africans were kidnapped, shipped to the colonies, and sold into slavery. Millions died during the passage. Others died in slavery.

Owners considered slaves property, yet treated slaves worse than they would their tools or animals. Slaves were raped, tortured, chained, and subjected to other inhumane treatment. They were intimidated, threatened, and killed to keep them docile and to control other slaves. Most slaves also were prevented from learning how to read and write. Owners feared that slaves would be able to escape—or revolt—if they were educated.

Most owners forbade slaves to marry. Yet they forced slaves to have sexual relations, breeding them like animals to increase the number of slaves. Like their parents, slave children were the property of their owner.

The Civil War began in 1861. Slavery was a key factor fueling the four-year conflict. By its end, slavery had been outlawed. Yet racism continued. A series of laws

Blacks endured various forms of racist behavior because of discriminatory Jim Crow laws that allowed unequal treatment in public places such as bus stations.

called Jim Crow laws were passed that discriminated against blacks. They enforced segregation, causing blacks to endure unjust, unequal treatment.

The civil rights movement helped end those laws. It led to the passage of several new laws. The Civil Rights Act of 1964 bans discrimination based on race and other factors. Other laws that came out of the civil rights movement include the Voting Rights Act of 1965 and the Civil Rights Acts of 1968 (which banned housing discrimination).

OPPRESSED NATIVE AMERICANS

Even as blacks were enslaved, Native Americans continually encountered widespread racism. One of the reasons is that they were considered inferior, partly because some native peoples' traditional way of life did not depend on farming and land management. And they lived on lands that whites wanted—badly. White Americans kept taking over more and more land, yet Native Americans still

FAKE NEWS

Fake news is any false information masquerading as real. When people read it, many can't tell it is untrue. For example, according to a study by Common Sense Media, 44 percent of kids cannot tell what news source is fake or real. That's a problem.

Teens who don't have the critical-thinking skills to tell the difference can be tricked into believing false stories, including those about another race. Those stories already cause division and make people angry. If you believe them, you, too, can be involved in sharing or reacting to false material. Don't be fooled!

Check headlines, website links (URLs), spelling, and the source to know if a story is legitimate. Also note if it calls itself satire. A form of humor, satire is similar to a joke. It is untrue. Many schools now teach teens how to identify fake news using these and other methods. If you find fake news online, don't believe it. Report any seen on social media.

occupied territory that whites wanted. Whites saw their presence as an obstruction.

The Indian Removal Act of 1830 helped white settlers take more land. The act called for five tribes to be removed from areas in the southeastern United States to reservations in Oklahoma. In other words, they were forced into isolation.

The removal of Native Americans began in 1831 and ended seven years later. The trek to Oklahoma was about one thousand miles (1,610 km) and took six months, mostly by foot! It became known as the Trail of Tears because of the suffering and deaths that occurred. Of those who made the journey, 25 percent—or one in four people—died as they traveled to the reservation.

THE IMPACT OF 9/11

Nearly three thousand people died during the terrorist attacks on the World Trade Center and the Pentagon on September 11, 2001. The nineteen attackers who hijacked the four airplanes were members of al-Qaeda, an Islamic group known for its extreme views. The horrific event shocked the world. It also changed how the United States and the world dealt with terrorism.

Unfortunately, in the United States and abroad many people of Muslim, Arab, and South Asian backgrounds experienced a spike in racist behavior after 9/11. Citizens, visitors, and immigrants were victims of racial profiling. Many were treated with suspicion. Others encountered racial slurs and physical attacks in schools, workplaces,

Since 9/11, there have been several attacks against Sikhs. This vigil was held after a white supremacist opened fire at a Sikh temple in Oak Creak, Wisconsin, in 2012.

and other places in their communities. Many were afraid to show signs of their religion or culture, including the special clothing worn in observance of their faith.

MORE TARGETS

Over the years, other targets have included people of Chinese, Japanese, Southeast Asian, and Hispanic descent. They, too, have endured jokes about their races, cultures, languages, and more. Similarly, they have been shut out of jobs and denied housing. Their children have been ridiculed and bullied in school.

The Chinese Exclusion Act of 1882 banned most immigration from China. It was the first federal law to bar the entry of people into the United States based on their ethnicity. In the midst of the Great Depression, more than one million Mexican Americans, a majority of whom were American citizens, were either coerced or involuntarily deported to Mexico. During World War II, Japanese Americans were confined to internment camps under the suspicion that they were loyal to Japan. Despite the fact that the United States was also fighting against Germany and Italy, German Americans and Italian Americans were never treated in anything approaching a similar way.

TRAVELING TIPS

Many minorities experience high levels of discrimination while traveling. They are subjected to racist behavior that ranges from mild to violent. Here are some tips on dealing with racist behavior while traveling:

- Report racist behavior to the appropriate authorities.
- Comply with police instructions when pulled over during a traffic stop.
- Record conversations when possible.
- Report racist behavior in a store to a retailer's corporate headquarters.
- Share your experience on social media. Social media has been effective in helping to share reports of racist behavior, bringing about justice in many cases.

IMMIGRATION POLICIES

Every country has its own policy regarding immigration. Each policy addresses immigrants and refugees. Immigrants and refugees are people who migrate to other countries. Immigrants are people who come for various reasons. They are often looking for a better way of life. They sometimes have family living in the country to which they want to migrate. Refugees are people who flee a country in turmoil. Key reasons people leave their homeland include religious persecution, racism, and political upheaval. Many also flee in times of war, famine, natural disasters, financial devastation, violence (including gang wars), and other conditions.

Immigration policies detail the reasons noncitizens can lawfully enter a country for prolonged stays. Each also includes the consequences for illegal entry into a country. In times of war, famine, political upheaval, religious persecution, and other crises, some countries will ease their policies to help people who are fleeing their native countries.

When parents flee, they take their children with them. Some never go through the formal process of complying with immigration policies. Because they do not have the official paperwork, these people are known as undocumented immigrants. Many go through formal procedures to become citizens, others never do. Undocumented immigrants have come under fire in recent years as immigration policies have been designed to locate them and return them to their native countries.

Changing immigration policies are a concern for many immigrants. Tony Solis, who had been protected under the Deferred Action for Childhood Arrivals (DACA) program, worried when the program was ended in 2017.

How do immigration policies relate to racism? Basically, immigration policies are designed to benefit each respective country while offering a humane solution to the problem of worldwide crises. But many people have argued that these same policies can be used as a tool for racism. In fact, they have done just that time and time again.

Regardless of a person's place of birth, no one should have to endure racism. Teens confront racist behavior when they stand up to those who tease, torment, or hurt other people because of their race.

CHAPTER FOUR

CONFRONTING RACIST BEHAVIOR

V ictims of racism often hear taunts like, "where do you come from?"; "you're not welcome here!"; or "go back to your country!"

Challenging a person's citizenship hits at a core aspect of that person's identity. Such comments undermine victims' pride in being American. They make victims feel as if they will never matter in the United States.

Former president Barack Obama dealt with such attacks. A rumor claimed he was not born in the United States. His presidency made many minorities hope for better race relations. Yet he could not escape racism! The attacks on him proved again the need to confront racism.

What does it mean to confront a social issue? To confront means to challenge, defy, or oppose. It also means to tackle or fight. Concerned citizens can include people from every walk of life and from every racial group. They can be adults, children, or teens.

In order to confront racist behavior, you first need to be able to identify what you are challenging, defying, opposing, or fighting. Then you can choose how to confront it. You can work alone or with groups. People oppose racism in different ways. These methods can be positive or negative. People may not agree as to which an individual act falls under. Residents may view a peaceful rally as negative because it reveals the racism in a community. That does not make it negative. Americans have the right to assemble peacefully.

How do you know if your approach is positive? Ask:

- Is it peaceful?
- Does it oppose or support bias?
- Does it demean anyone?
- Is it violent?

Nonviolence is always positive. Various methods of nonviolent protest exist. These include marches, rallies, voter registration drives, prayer vigils, and boycotts.

Prayer vigils are one peaceful way to protest racist behavior. This vigil was held in Arlington, Texas, after a white supremacist opened fire in a black church in Charleston, South Carolina, in 2015.

CREATIVITY ON THE FRONTLINES

Today, the internet offers a quick and easy way to oppose racist behavior. People use social media platforms to immediately respond to situations in the United States and around the world. Ordinary citizens views have been aired, shared, and used to demonstrate the consensus that racism is wrong and should not be tolerated—anywhere!

Websites can also be a way to oppose racism. For example, the teen activist Ziad Ahmed created the website redefy.org. Ahmed is a Muslim American who

Redefy Founder and President Ziad Ahmed, a Muslim American teen activist, is shown (far right) with some of the team members of his successful website.

has fought racism and bias for years. The site is a place for teen activists to speak out against injustice, including racism. Teens who serve as officers and contributors are citizens from America and abroad.

DARE TO BE DIFFERENT

Retaliation is a form of negative confrontation. It could occur when someone hurls a racist insult, punches, or otherwise hurts you, and you respond with equal or greater fury or force. Such actions make it difficult to differentiate a racist from an activist. They have consequences. You could be arrested, suspended from school, physically hurt, or even killed.

Taking advantage of peaceful demonstrations can also be negative. Some people turn these into opportunities for violence or theft. Harming people and property is not the way to achieve justice. Don't do it! Looting is a crime. Teens who loot, damage property, or steal during a crisis are lawbreakers. Do not mirror the actions of the very people whose behavior you oppose. Dare to be different! Use positive means of confronting racism.

WHY BOTHER?

Youth diversity is increasing. As diversity increases, so does the need to protect the rights and lives of minorities of all ages given the history of racism and prejudice against racial minorities in the United States.

The world is also diverse, and minorities face challenges worldwide. That is the bad news. The good news is that many opportunities exist for young people to confront racist behavior. Why bother getting involved? Your involvement helps:

- address and fight injustice
- tear down walls of separation
- build bridges to peace
- promote acceptance of diverse people
- build a better today and tomorrow

DEFYING RACISM

In recent years, the response to racism has been swift. A series of racially motivated police-involved murders have shaken the nation. These have prompted outcry. People have demanded that cases be investigated and that any involved officer be stripped of their duties. Unfortunately, this has not always been the case. Instead, in numerous cases, police have been exonerated, whether they were declared not guilty in a court of law or protected from prosecution.

Concerned American citizens have used a variety of means to confront this issue. For example, the Black Lives Matter movement formed to address violence and racist behavior against blacks. It has brought the issue of excessive police brutality to the forefront of discussions centered on race and equality.

Black Lives Matter supporters gathered at the place where Walter Scott was shot and killed in Charleston, and they also attended a press conference about the incident.

Black Lives Matter supporters have protested numerous deaths of black people who were killed during encounters with the police, and especially in cases in which the police were later cleared of any crime. Some of those include the 2014 murders of Michael Brown in Ferguson, Missouri, and Eric Garner in New York City.

BRINGING DOWN MONUMENTS

In the past few years, white hate groups have become more active. They have staged rallies and conducted speeches on college campuses and in other places.

BIRTH OF A MOVEMENT

In 2012, a black teenager named Trayvon Martin was shot and killed by a multiracial man named George Zimmerman. At the time, Zimmerman was part of a neighborhood watch group in Sanford, Florida. After the incident, people took to social media and discussed their concerns using the hashtag #blacklivesmatter.

The hashtag was used repeatedly. It helped birth the Black Lives Matter movement. This campaign highlights racist behavior that harms or kills African Americans. It has been successful in making the country—and the world—aware of racist behavior that might otherwise go unreported. Supporters continually emphasize the need for consequences for unlawful behavior.

Critics, however, believe that the movement's name, mission, and actions are racist. They think it stresses that only black lives matter. Those critics are misinformed. That is not the movement's message or mission.

In response, antiracism supporters have shown up to protest these rallies. Their presence makes it clear that some communities do not welcome racist behavior.

For example, in August 2017 a rally was held in Charlottesville, Virginia. It was organized by hate groups. They gathered to protest the city's plan to remove a statute of Robert E. Lee. He was a general during the Civil War for the Confederacy, the states that wanted to keep slavery and split from the Union to try to do so.

Heather Heyer, a white woman, was killed and other counterprotestors were injured when a white

People gather at the Charlottesville, Virginia, site where a white supremacist drove into the crowd, killed Heather Heyer, and injured others like Marcus Martin (*seated*).

supremacist drove into the crowd. The driver was arrested and charged with her murder. However, the event sparked nationwide outrage. It also inspired the removal of similar monuments around the country.

Racism persists because of hatred and ignorance. Many people fight for causes that are not rooted in knowledge, but ignorance. Their efforts do not achieve their desired results—and may actually hinder their cause—because they are confronting the wrong issue, problem, or group. Understanding that racist behavior is exhibited in multiple ways helps teens better confront it.

10 GREAT QUESTIONS TO ASK A COMMUNITY ACTIVIST

1. What inspired you to become an activist, and what inspires you to confront racism?
2. How do current events affect your job?
3. Have you ever been a victim of racism?
4. What factors make your role difficult?
5. What are some of the racial challenges communities face today?
6. How do you work with law enforcement to address issues in your community?
7. How can teens become involved in community activism?
8. Do you ever get afraid while helping fight racism?
9. How can I help fight racism at school?
10. How can I help my family understand the importance of confronting racist behavior?

CHAPTER FIVE

GAME CHANGERS

Today, activists increasingly call for other Americans to be "woke" concerning racism. The term means to be aware of racist behavior and to address it as it happens. Woke teens are game changers. They acknowledge that racism exists and find ways to address it as best they can.

Teens can—and do—make a difference. You can confront racist behavior in some way. You can put your desire for social justice to good use. Discover ways you can help. Then choose those that are best suited to you, given your interests, resources, talents, and available time. These may be different from those your friends engage in. That's OK.

CHECK YOURSELF

Before you begin, check yourself. It is easy to point the finger at other people and spotlight their demeaning attitudes or actions. It's more difficult to take a closer look at yourself. But it is necessary.

Personal reflection and answering tough questions can help identify and eliminate any biases that could hinder your ability to effectively confront racist behavior.

What harmful biases do you have? How do you treat people who are not like you and what assumptions do you make about them? Do you make supposedly funny jokes that ridicule members of other races? Do you sometimes despise your hair, skin color, facial features, or other characteristics? If you are a multiracial teen, do you sometimes hide or deny a part of your identity?

These are tough questions. Yet it is important for teens to answer them. Doing so will help teens check themselves, a necessary first step in helping confront racism.

Checking yourself also includes developing a positive self-image. If you struggle with suicidal thoughts, low self-esteem, or low self-confidence because of racist treatment you have experienced or witnessed, get assistance. Speak with a guidance counselor, parent or guardian, or other trusted adult. Speak honestly about any suicidal feelings so you get prompt help. Request strategies and resources for improving your self-esteem and self-confidence. You will not be an effective game changer until you fully embrace your identity, including your racial uniqueness.

STAY WOKE

Staying woke entails courageously acknowledging and reporting racist behavior. You have probably heard the slogan "If you see something, say something" many times. It encourages people to report criminal activity to law enforcement personnel or other authority figures. How can you use the slogan as an antiracism tool?

Discuss the issue. Discussions about racism can be difficult. That does not mean the topic should be tabled. Rather, it is essential to discuss it. Engage in positive discussions with peers, educators, and activists. Ask questions. Share your experiences. Be open minded and honest. Be willing to learn, grow, and change based on the formal and informal discussions you have with others.

Speak up. Report all racist behavior you see or hear. At school, speak with a guidance counselor, school administrator, educator, or other staff member. Explain what happened, and the parties involved. Be specific. Detailed reports make it easier to identify, catch, or disci-

Joining a school organization is a way to stay woke by discussing the issues and engaging in activities that confront racist behavior.

pline those involved. In the community, take your concern to whoever is in authority. In a retail store, report racist activity to a manager or member of a security team. For example, be courageous and report your gut feeling that you were racially profiled while shopping. Explain what occurred.

Report all bullying. Support victims by reporting bullying, including racially motivated behavior. Do not protect friends who engage in such actions.

Respect others' experiences. You may not understand why, or agree with, others' views, opinions, or fears. That's understandable if you have not experienced the same humiliating treatment. Thus do not mock or treat another teen's concerns lightly. Rather, respect them!

Serve as a peer mediator. Peer mediators are key student leaders who help resolve conflicts arising in school between students. The role helps teens develop conflict-resolution skills. Those skills are useful in addressing all types of conflict, including racist behavior in and out of school.

Celebrate appropriately. Some people use holidays, especially Halloween, to promote their racist agendas. Others incorporate racist themes in their birthday parties and other "celebrations." Stay woke. Do not engage in any activity that reinforces stereotypes or promotes prejudice.

Donate or help raise money. Money is needed to help fund organizations and events that confront racism. Consider donating money you receive from allowances or your part-time job wages. Help raise funds by joining community or social media fund-raising campaigns.

ENGAGE IN ACTIVISM

Racism is evil. It destroys people, communities, and nations. Take a stand. Engage in activism to confront racist behavior. Activists have long played important roles in fighting injustice. Try adopting one of the more successful methods. For example, attend an antiracism or diversity program sponsored by your school, local library, religious organization, a corporation, or other concerned group. Join school organizations that help promote racial tolerance and acceptance. If this kind of organization doesn't exist at your school, consider founding one.

READ TO LEAD

Reading is one way to become more informed about race relations. Some options to explore are:

- Novels and short stories. For example, the Black Lives Matter movement is central to the 2017 novel *The Hate U Give* by Angie Thomas.
- Poetry, such as that of bell hooks.
- Biographies and autobiographies about people who confronted racism, such as Ta-Nehisi Coates's memoir *Between the World and Me*.
- Articles in newspaper and magazines and on websites and blogs of reliable news sources.

Where to start? Ask a teacher or school librarian for suggestions. Visit your local library. Ask about new releases for teens. Also ask about readings or book signings that might provide a chance to hear from activists or authors who confront racism. Finally, talk with friends and family about what they read to stay inspired.

Team up with family. If you've heard about an event you want to attend, invite your family to come too. If a family member's job is hosting a special observation or program, ask that person if you can attend. If you have family members who are guilty of racist behavior or comments, confront them about it. Share why it is offensive, and request that it cease. Know that you may need help from a parent or other trusted relative during this confrontation.

Use reliable sources to stay informed, and share only reliable information. Make use of social media to responsibly address current events and to participate in special campaigns. For example, the Yes, You're Racist Twitter account sparked outrage after the August 2017 Charlottesville, Virginia, incident. The creators posted pictures of racists who had participated in the event and asked for the public's help in identifying them. The social media campaign worked! Twitter users shared pictures to their accounts and asked for their followers' help. Responses began pouring in. The result? Some of those identified faced consequences in their jobs or at their schools.

VOLUNTEER

Activism works because people volunteer their time, talent, and resources to help. Seek out volunteer opportunities at your school or with other community organizations. Needs can vary. Volunteers are often needed to assist with telephone campaigns, print material distribution, special events, social media messaging, and many other activities. In truth, most organizations' need for volunteers tends to be greater than the number of willing workers.

Remember to seek volunteer opportunities that are of high interest to you or that match your skills. If you like graphic arts, helping design posters, flyers, or other print media may be an especially rewarding volunteer gig. Serving on an event's tech staff is a way to use your technical skills in music or video production. If you have a heart for helping people in other countries, you may be interested in organizations that sponsor service or mission trips abroad.

CULTURAL EXCHANGES

Whether in the United States or abroad, such trips provide cultural exchanges that help teens become more familiar with people outside of their race or culture. This is key as, again, ignorance often breeds racism. However, knowledge can lead to acceptance and respect.

There are other ways teens can become more familiar with teens of other races. You can 1) make diverse friends; 2) promote understanding of your race and/or culture; 3) learn a foreign language so you can communicate with non-English speaking peers; or 4) use your bilingual skills to provide tutoring or interpreting assistance at school or in the community.

Hate is a way of life for some people and their families and friends. They introduce children and teens to their vile way of life. Staunch racists also recruit college students. These facts might be a wake-up call for teens who may believe exposure to racist behavior ends when they reach a certain age.

LOOKING FORWARD

People often talk about their dream for national or global peace. In his famous "I Have a Dream" speech,

Martin Luther King Jr. expressed his. He said, "I have a dream that my four little children will one day live in a nation where they will not be judged by the color of their skin but by the content of their character."

Long after King was murdered, his dream has yet to be realized in the United States. Innocent people are still being murdered because of their race. Minorities are still being negatively judged by their skin color rather than their character. So what's the bottom line? Change is still needed. Hatred, fear, and ignorance are key reasons why racism persists. Regardless of its type or intensity, racist behavior harms victims. Each victim is affected in different ways. They need friends, family, and strangers to work for positive change.

When people of all races come together to confront racism, they spark shared healing. When teens get involved, they help build communities where tolerance and acceptance prospers. In such areas, residents resist poor treatment of their neighbors and fight to reduce racism wherever it tries to raise its head.

Confronting racist behavior is not a one-time deal. It starts with confronting one's own biases. Then it requires courage to stand up for what is right, even in the face of opposition from family and friends. It also requires making an important decision.

What makes one person confront social issues, while another does not? Sometimes it is because the first person is passionate about the issue and wants to be part of the solution. At times, it may be because the second person does not feel they can contribute much to the solution or does not know how. Other times, that

There are many ways to become involved in confronting racist behavior. Your efforts assure that you have a choice in shaping a better future for people of all races.

second person is simply unbothered because the issue doesn't affect them.

It is a cliché, but also true that children are a nation's future. You represent a future member of society. Only you can choose whether you will become a racist, a bystander, or an activist. Today, choose to be a game changer. Choose to begin using your skills, talent, intellect, and other resources to help foster racial harmony. Choose to confront racist behavior.

GLOSSARY

bias A prejudice, preference, or opinion that subjects someone to undesirable treatment.

boycott A type of protest that encourages people not to use a service or buy a product.

civil rights movement Organized protests during the 1950s and 1960s that were designed to force the end of segregation in the United States.

coerce To manipulate a person into doing something they do not want to do.

consensus An agreement among people about something, such as the cause or outcome of an issue.

demean To humiliate or degrade a person or group.

deport To send someone to another country, often to the country from which that person initially came.

discrimination Subjecting someone to unfair or unequal treatment based on a predetermined factor, such as race, gender, or economic status (class).

indentured servants Workers who hired themselves out for a certain time.

Jim Crow laws Laws existing from the 1890s until the 1960s that discriminated against blacks and forced them to be segregated from whites.

looting Stealing from homes or stores during a time of unrest, such as a riot or a natural disaster.

noose A rope hung from a tree that symbolizes the murders of blacks who were killed by hanging. Nooses are symbols of racism and used to scare, threaten, and intimidate blacks.

police brutality The use of excessive force by police when dealing with members of the community.

prejudice A synonym of bigotry, it is a narrow-minded, preconceived, uninformed, and negative opinion about a person or group that results in discrimination.

racial profiling Suspecting a person of wrongdoing based on that person's race or ethnicity.

segregation Separating people, especially by race.

simplistic Overly simplified.

swastika A symbol used by the Nazi Party in Germany that became associated with the mass killings of Jewish people and white supremacy.

tolerance Attitudes and actions that reflect respect and acceptance of people regardless of their race, gender, religion, sexual orientation, gender identity, or other status.

vigil An evening service designed to unite a community or protest an event or issue that has negatively impacted that community.

white supremacist A person who thinks white people are superior to those of other races and should therefore lead society.

FOR MORE INFORMATION

Amnesty International Canada
312 Laurier Avenue E
Ottawa, ON K1N 1H9
Canada
(613) 744-7667
Website: hllp://www.amnesty.ca
Facebook: @amnestycanada
Twitter: @AmnestyNow
Dedicated to fighting injustice and promoting human
    rights, Amnesty International was founded in 1961 and
    works in countries around the world.

Multicultural Council of Saskatchewan
452 Albert Street North
Regina, SK S4R 3C1
Treaty 4 Territory
Homeland of the Métis
Canada
(306) 721-6267
Website: http://mcos.ca
Facebook: @MulticulturalCouncilofSK
Twitter: @MC_o_S
Dedicated to supporting multiculturalism in Canada, the
    council offers various resources, including training for
    Anti-Racism Youth Leadership Workshops.

Smithsonian National Museum of African American
    History & Culture
1400 Constitution Ave NW

Washington, DC 20560
(844) 750-3012
Website: https://nmaahc.si.edu
Facebook/Twitter: @NMAAHC
This museum in Washington, DC, on the National Mall,
opened in 2016 and had more than one million visitors
in its first six months.

Southern Poverty Law Center
400 Washington Avenue
Montgomery, AL 36104
(334) 956-8200 or Toll-Free at (888) 414-7752
Website: https://www.splcenter.org
Facebook: @SPLCenter
Twitter: @splcenter
An organization that monitors hate group activity, pro-
motes tolerance, and advocates for justice.

What Kids Can Do
PO Box 603252
Providence, RI 02906
(401) 247-7665
Website: http://www.whatkidscando.org
This nonprofit organization focuses on sharing inspiration-
al and informative videos, free publications, and other
resources (including other related websites) that help
kids understand what they can do regarding social
issues.

FOR FURTHER READING

Aretha, David. *Out in Front: Malala Yousafzai and the Girls of Pakistan.* Greensboro, NC: Morgan Reynolds Publishing, 2014.

Coates, Ta-Nehisi. *Between the World and Me.* New York, NY: Spiegel & Grau, 2015.

Gitlin, Marty. *Combatting Discrimination Against Women in the Gamer Community.* New York, NY: Rosen Publishing, 2017.

Grinapol, Corinne. *Racial Profiling and Discrimination: Your Legal Rights.* New York, NY: Enslow Publishing, 2016.

Hanson-Harding, Alexandra. *Are You Being Racially Profiled?* (Got Issues?). New York, NY: Enslow Publishing, 2016.

Hilton, Marilyn. *Full Cicada Moon.* New York, NY: Penguin Group, 2015.

Perkins, Matali, ed. *Open Mic: Riffs on Life Between Cultures in Ten Voices.* Somerville, MA: Candlewick Press, 2013.

Thomas, Angie. *The Hate U Give.* New York, NY: Balzer + Bray, 2017.

Tonatiuh, Duncan. *Separate Is Never Equal: Sylvia Mendez & Her Family's Fight for Desegregation.* New York, NY: Abrams, 2014.

Williams-Garcia, Rita. *Gone Crazy in Alabama.* New York, NY: Amistad, 2015.

Woodson, Jacqueline. *Brown Girl Dreaming.* New York, NY: Penguin Group, 2014.

BIBLIOGRAPHY

ACT (Assets Coming Together) for Youth Center of Excellence. "U.S. Teen Demographics." Retrieved July 29, 2017. http://www.actforyouth.net/adolescence /demographics.

American Psychological Association. "Is It You or Is It Racist? The Insidious Impact of Microaggressions on Mental Health." July 31, 2013. https:// psychologybenefits.org/2013/07/31/is-it-you-or-is-it -racist-the-insidious-impact-of-microaggressions -on-mental-health.

Anti-Defamation League. "10 Ways Youth Can Engage In Activism." Retrieved July 17, 2017. https://www .adl.org/education/resources/tools-and-strategies /10-ways-youth-can-engage-in-activism.

Colby, Sandra L., and Jennifer M. Ortman, "Projections of the Size and Composition of the U.S. Population: 2014 to 2060." United States Census Bureau. March 2015. census.gov/content/dam/Census/library /publications/2015/demo/p25-1143.pdf.

Common Sense Media. "Do tweens and teens believe 'fake news'?" Retrieved September 4, 2017. https:// www.commonsensemedia.org/news -and-media-literacy/do-tweens-and-teens-believe -fake-news#.

Crabtree, Steve. "Do Teens 'Clique' With Diversity." Gallup. December 16, 2002. http://www.gallup.com /poll/10219/teens-clique-diversity.aspx.

Haugen, Hayley Mitchell, ed. *Social Issues Firtshand: Racism.* Farmington Hills, MI: Greenhaven Press, 2008.

King, Martin Luther, Jr. *A Time to Break Silence. The Essential Works of Martin Luther King Jr. for Students.* Meyers, Walter Dean, ed. Boston, MA: Beacon Press, 2013.

Kite, Mary E. "Microaggression Activity." Retrieved September 9, 2017. http://breakingprejudice.org /teaching/group-activities/microaggression-activity.

Luscombe, Belinda. "More Than Half of American Kids Say They Can't Spot Fake News." *Time*, March 8, 2017. http://time.com/4694165/more-than-half-of -kids-say-they-cant-spot-fake-news.

PBS NewsHour. "Inspired by internment camp history, students write a musical work and hear echoes of today." April 13, 2017. http://www.pbs.org/newshour /bb/inspired-internment-camp-history-students -write-musical-work-hear-echoes-today.

Peacock, Thomas, and Marlene Wisuri. *To Be Free: Understanding and Eliminating Racism.* Afton, MN: Afton Press, 2010.

Root, The. "4 Things to Tell Teens Who Joke About Race." January 8, 2014. https://www.theroot.com/4- things-to-tell-teens-who-joke-about-race -1790874035.

Southern Poverty Law Center. "Hate Map." Retrieved September 5, 2017. https://www.splcenter.org /hate-map.

Southern Poverty Law Center. "Ten Ways to Fight Hate: A Community Response Guide." Fifth Edition, Au-

gust 14, 2017. https://www.splcenter.org/20170814
/ten-ways-fight-hate-community-response-guide.

Teen Talk. "Diversity and Discrimination." Retrieved July
29, 2017. http://teentalk.ca/hot-topics/appreciating
-diversity-2.

Toppo, Greg. "Growing up 'post-racial,' teens suddenly
find a world that isn't." *USA Today*. December 10,
2014. https://www.usatoday.com/story/news/nation
/2014/12/10/teen-attitudes-race-diversity-america
/19749199.

U.S. Department of Health & Human Services. "The
Changing Face of America's Adolescents." Retrieved July 29, 2017. https://www.hhs.gov/ash/oah
/facts-and-stats/changing-face-of-americas
-adolescents/index.html.

Walker, John. "These 7 Microaggressions Could Ruin
Someone's Day." MTV News. July 14, 2017. http://
www.mtv.com/news/1871828/look-different
-microaggression-videos.

Weber, Diane, and Laurie Mandel. *Totally Tolerant:
Spotting and Stopping Prejudice.* New York, NY:
Franklin Watts, 2008.

West, Cornel. *Race Matters.* New York, NY: Vintage
Books, 1994.

INDEX

ABOUT THE AUTHOR

A former corporate publications editor and writer, Lisa A. Crayton loves writing for children and teens. She is the author or coauthor of several books for youth. She loves mentoring writers and especially enjoys speaking at writers' conferences. She earned a master of fine arts degree from National University and a bachelor's degree in public relations and journalism, cum laude, from Utica College.

PHOTO CREDITS